AQUAMARINE

Ken Beevers

AQUAMARINE

Ken Beevers

Poetry Island Press

Copyright © Ken Beevers 2019

Front cover designed by Brian Mills www.bmillsdesigns.co.uk
Front cover Copyright © Ken Beevers/Poetry Island Press 2019
Back cover photo of Ken Beevers Copyright © Ian Beech 2017
Back cover logo Copyright © Poetry Island Press/Jo Mortimer 2015
For additional Credits and Copyright information see Pages 85-86

The author asserts the moral right under the Copyright, Designs and Patents Act 1988 to be identified as the author of this work.

All rights reserved. No part of this publication may be reproduced, stored in a retrieval system, or transmitted, in any form or by any means without the prior written consent of Poetry Island Press, nor be otherwise circulated in any form of binding or cover other than that in which it is published and without a similar condition being imposed on the subsequent purchaser.

This edition published by Poetry Island Press 2019

Poetry Island Press
29 Dean Street, Crediton, EX17 3EN

ISBN 978-0-9933961-1-3

Every effort has been made to locate owners of any copyright material used in this book. The author apologises for any omissions. Those brought to the author's attention will be incorporated in future editions.

Printed by www.lulu.com

For Jacqui and all Poetry Islanders

I would particularly like to thank Ian Beech for his constant encouragement, for suggesting I merited a book, and for offering to publish it under the Poetry Island Press imprint. I am very proud of that. He has taken great care and time putting it together, been very patient, and offered helpful advice throughout, in addition to real friendship and support through a difficult time. On behalf of all Poetry Islanders I would like to thank him for some memorable nights of spoken word. Special thanks also to Robert Garnham for boosting my confidence and for the laughs, and to Chris Brooks for his enthusiastic tutoring. I am very grateful to my mentors Sam Watson and Chris Woodhouse at South Devon College, for their help and that all important first bit of constructive criticism and appreciation. Thanks to all my friends in poetry, POETS Friday, Paignton Writing Circle, Jon Brooks, tutor Katie Sloane and my fellow students at Paignton Library. And thank you to Simon Pitt, a former Bard of Birmingham, for an inspiring glimpse into performing back in 1989 at Breightmet Library, Bolton. I am sorry it is a bit late. Saul Bellow cautioned that people could lose their lives in libraries and should be warned. Jacqui Beevers knows all about that. Thanks to her for love and understanding.

Foreword

The moment I heard Ken Beevers perform *Everyone Likes the Sound of Their Own Name*, I thought there was something special about him. On that memorable Poetry Island evening at The Blue Walnut in 2014, not only was I impressed by Ken and his poem but I thought there was something familiar about the sound of his name too. The following month, during his set, Ken mentioned that he was a former librarian and my suspicions were confirmed! We soon established that we had known each other thirty years earlier, sitting on the national committee of a Library Association group. Later, Ken unearthed the published photograph of us, relatively youthful participants in an impromptu football match at a library conference in Southport in May 1984. As you may imagine, neither of us has aged one jot during the intervening years.

Please forgive this self-indulgent nostalgia but meeting Ken again after all those years was an amazing coincidence and a great stroke of luck.

Over the last five years, I have had the immense pleasure of getting to know Ken extremely well, programming him at numerous poetry events and watching his writing and performance skills blossom in the warmth of audience appreciation.

It is a real honour and a privilege to publish Ken's amazing book. There is so much to savour and admire in this brilliant first collection. In the title poem of *AQUAMARINE*, Ken demonstrates his playful love of words and language, launching us into a feast of writing.

The book is full of warmth, tenderness and sensitivity and, through his great love of nature and countryside walks, Ken invites us to ramble with him through the highways and byways of his cultured mind. He has a wonderful ability to evoke the glories of the past. This is a book full of memories: while it would be inaccurate to say that Ken lives in the past, he certainly has a season ticket to revisit it as and when he pleases.

Ken is a highly-talented poet and storyteller who deserves a blue plaque of his very own. He needn't worry about trying '*to shine,/ Look pale and interesting*': he's not pale, his words captivate and he is stellar bright. I'm sure you'll enjoy his book.

Ian Beech

Contents

AQUAMARINE	11
Cyan	12
The World's Narrowest Street	13
Slinkers Lane	14
Johnny Onions	15
The Palisaded Palm	16
Safe Passage	17
The Secret Seamstress	19
Hands	21
Cycling City	22
Mondays	23
Everyone Likes the Sound of Their Own Name	24
How to Make Yourself Disappear	25
Illumination	26
Message	26
Rich Man in His Castle	27
Bertie Lewis	28
Poetry Island Discs	30
Tattoos of Tenderness	32
I Love Paris Road	33
Just Desserts	34
A Garden's Lament	35
That Summer	36
On the Warren	37
The John Charles Stamp	38
Man Lying on a Wall, 1957, By L. S. Lowry	39
The Eternal Triangle	41
White Dress	42
The Battle of Spittle Street	43
The Date	46
Bullsh*t	49
Rogue's Treasures	50
The Old School Ties	51
John Brodie Lived Here	53
The Lost Art of Goalpost Chalking	54
Planet Earth Diary	55
The Rose Bowl	58
The Clotted Cream Diaries	59
The Greatest Shakespearean	61
The Light of the World	62

The Blow-In	63
Walking the St. Swithun's Way, July 2012	64
Priceless	65
I Was Reading	66
Bonjour Tristesse	68
Don't Get Mad, Get Even	69
Shirt Tale	70
At Atcham, by Hotel and Church	72
Owd Chummy	73
Stanley Has an Off Day	75
A Secret Love	77
The World's Best Haiku	79
Notes	81
Illustrations and Credits	85
About the Author	87

AQUAMARINE

We had words last night.
She started it.
We talked of work,
The hours that dragged like trailing ropes,
Then the headlines of the news.
Something had to offer hope.
So after tea, craving beauty,
She said *'aquamarine'*,
And the colours of sea glass
Bathed our drab settee.

'Jacaranda'. Silence ...
How I love our silences,
Like *'syllabub'* and *'velvet'*,
All these erased the day's
Casual profanities.

Why swear when you can be sublime?
Shout *'shimmer'* at your football team,
'Tranquillity' and *'butterfly'*,
To all MPs on *Question Time*.
Curse your computer with *'celandine'*,
Or *'marigold'* or *'filigree'*.
'Akimbo' and *'flamingo'* will bewilder referee,
'Truffle' and *'kerfuffle'*, those who run the line.
My turn to get a word in,
Hers to write them down.

'Antimacassar and *mellifluous,*
Flamboyant and *Plantagenet,*
And *auburn*, oh ... *auburn.*
This town needs attractive words like that.
Onomatopoeia and *doppelgänger.'*

'You know I can't spell,
You *scrimshanker*!'

'*Xylophone* and *Pharaoh.*'

'*Nincompoop.*
Amaryllis.
Marshmallow.'

'*Beloved*' ...

'*Caress*' ...

'*Tingle*' ...

'*Lullaby.*'

Last night we had an exchange of words,
My love and I.

Cyan

On the old town road, at the bottom of the hill,
A strip of shops face an ancient inn.
Desire lines trace a punter's path
To its constant shining star, the Ocean Wild Fish Bar.
Spotless, stainless, burnished, recently refurbished
By an acolyte of Frank Lloyd Wright,
A gleaming Guggenheim satellite with Oscar-winning shop fitting
In every shade of cyan. Leicester socks and Radox bath
And Bristol glass, Cambridge, Carolina, royal blue of Aga.
A replica of Vegas but there's no sign of Elvis
Singing Blue Hawaii in a three bar harmony;
Public bar, nail bar and Ocean Wild Fish Bar.
Ethically supplied from seas never overfished,
The menu won the Pulitzer, but that's no surprise
With a range like a mighty Wurlitzer,
Computer-controlled with override, for fish cooked in tempura.
Every day is Friday, sunnier than pay day, savoury as a Saturday
At this utopian supper palace.
No need to go to Paris to feel adored and cherished,
For love in the queue there's a table for two,
The chip shop is suitably furnished.
Tête-à-tête, juxtaposed adjective and noun,
For stylish nutrition in our seaside town.

The World's Narrowest Street

In the prosperous, soft city on the Exe,
When the cheerfulness of teatime
Meets the switching on of lights,
An anxious murmuration starts to gather in the street,
Swirling round its tributaries,
No avenue unexplored,
Mingling with the monuments,
No stone is left unturned,
Weeping like the leaves from trees,
Then falling to the floor,
In any place that's sheltered,
And roughly in plain sight,
A bed of slabs to lie on,
Until the passing of the night.

Knees bent, heads down, backs against the wall.
Be grateful someone loves you when you close
Your own front door.

In the shadow of St Peter's,
When the cleansing of the morning,
Sweeps away the awful night,
A man becomes invisible,
And I condemn him for his countenance,
And desperate situation.
He sits beneath the plaque,
That says the world's narrowest street,
No purpose or horizons to help him to his feet.
He is trying to smooth his sleeping bag,
As if it was his life,
Hugging the logo on his chest,
For something to hold tight.

He looks right through my apathy,
To my selfish, hollow core.
'Have you never seen a homeless person?
Never been this close before?'

Knees bent, head down, nowhere else to fall.
Be grateful someone loves you when you close
Your own front door.

Slinkers Lane

I like to walk down Slinkers Lane,
Which twists and turns and twists again,
Behind the tangled woven hedge,
Of hawthorn, hornbeam, stick and sedge,
A lacework of converging ferns,
Still verdant when the season turns.
The rambling brambles scratch my eye,
I feel the pinch of midge and fly,
Stumble on the stones and fall,
Tripping over crumbling wall,
Rich in lichen, dripping mosses,
The verdigris of Dartmoor crosses.

I like to walk down Slinkers Lane,
Which twists and turns and twists again,
And elbows round the village fields,
A cloak of evergreen displays,
Which hide me with their foliage,
From any disapproving gaze,
Of those who plod to gate and church.
For I prefer the downward lurch,
To congregate in Kestor Inn,
Away from quiet Manaton.
I like to slip down Slinkers Lane,
And slink my way back home again.

Johnny Onions

Something has tainted the Christmas scene.
The nightmare posters of the UKIP dream
Have wormed their way into the struts and beams
Of the wooden huts on Cathedral Green.
Someone has stirred the pot, Madame,
And now you think I am a sham,
An alien, a ruffian,
A foreigner, a privateer.
You think my prices are too dear.
Your prejudice is so entrenched,
You don't think I'm really French,
I'm just a common marketeer
From a string of Onion Johns, Madame,
And I taste your indifference.
Let me tell you who I am, Madame.
My name is Johnny Onions, at your service.

I don't need a Breton top or black beret
To cook for you some tartiflette.
Look into the pan, Madame.
Potatoes waxy as you please,
Lashings of Reblochon cheese
And onions fresh from Brittany.
They never rot. They're pink of skin,
For centuries we have sailed them in,
And for these onions men have died,
Women grieved and children cried,
Bitter tears for the onion men,
Who never saw Roscoff again.

It's freezing here outside the nave,
But nothing like their channel grave.
I'm just a common marketeer.
Are my prices still too dear?
Écoutez la différence.
Let me tell you who I am. Madame,
My name is Johnny Onions, at your service.

The Palisaded Palm

Confined in black soil in a tiny terrace front garden,
In a wet street of a *Love on the Dole* sort of town,
A Torbay palm stretches and spreads
Among the chip shops and chimneys.

It casts no moving shadows on sunlit white walls,
And feels no salty spray. Its green lion's mane
Dark against Accrington brick, pressing for warmth
On small, sooted windows.

Once it sat on a young bride's lap, coming home
By train, from a wakes week Babbacombe honeymoon,
A gardener's gift, wrapped in newspaper,
And labelled with its Palm Sunday name,
Australis, a cordyline. Planted ceremoniously,
It boasted of time away from mill and mine.

On sunny days they sat on the stone step,
Watched the fronds waving memories,
Of linking arms on the Downs, or stretched
On the Abbey's glittering sands,
Beneath a smokeless sky.

Cream Egyptian sheets and teas, regatta fair,
Hills and peaks and sandstone walls,
With tumbling blue campanula, and street signs
Made of Minton tiles, spelling out
'Come back to us and honeymoon throughout your lives.'

But Glorious Devon remained just green hills far away
On a poster at the station. Now elegant white flowers
Adorn the palm's Golden Wedding day.
A new young wife sitting on the flat front step
Spills her tears on the flimsy letter in her lap,
From the home she left in Gujarat.
In the cold north wind, the palm dazzles and thrives,
Giving solace in this alien place, within its palisade.

Safe Passage

Going out is a rite of passage
Every parent has to manage.
First, preparation takes all evening,
Scrubbing, primping, posing, preening.

Then begins the living nightmare,
As daughters wearing flimsy nightwear,
And sons, who've never learned to fight,
Innocent, head out into the thrilling night.

You mustn't show them that you're scared
By lurid stories you have heard,
But tell them they look really nice,
In drooping pants and holey tights.

When you say you once were
Elton John's rightful heir,
They mock you, gently teasing, being funny,
Even as you give them folding money.

They promise not to be too late,
'Unless', they laugh, 'we land a mate.'
'Know what we mean, Rocket Man', they cry.
But you can't look them in the eye.

You make a joke to break the ice.
'Before the milkman would be nice.'
They kiss you, tell you not to fret.
'Don't wait up, don't get upset.

Please don't ring us up again,
Especially not at half past ten.
You've no idea the flak we got
From Jason Black and Mandy Trott.'

As soon as they go out the door
They're looking for someone, something more …

You touch the place where you've been kissed
And assume your role of fatalist.
The lonely ditch, the random fight,
Will terrorise your dreams tonight.

Babies only yesterday,
They swagger down the alleyway,
Bottle-feeding once again,
On Budweiser and Speckled Hen.

No longer wrapped in cotton wool,
They're on the lash and on the pull,
The cattle market monkey run,
Heading for delirium.

You hear the key, and then the door,
The kettle's reassssssssssuring roar.
Then the sign you love the most:
The intoxicating smell of toast.

It tells you they've not run aground,
Their passage has been safe and sound.
The lights go out and night descends,
But a parent's watch, it never ends.

The Secret Seamstress

Everybody knows,
Mothers are the ones who contribute most.
Fathers are flawed, some should even be
Recalled.

Our house was one of those,
With a mum without blemish,
Who was, in addition,
A dressmaking genius,
A marvellous machinist,

Who told us she made the space suits for the Apollo mission.

Look at her CV. She made more garments
Than the Lancashire textile industry,
Drainpiped my brother's trousers,
Dressed every bridesmaid in our street,
And sewed and hemmed its curtains,
Respectable and neat.

She spoke the poetry of sewing,
The language of selvage and overlays,
Letting out and taking in.
She was fluent in broderie anglaise,
Even with a mouth full of pins.

She loved a man in uniform,
But only for his warp and weft.
She stitched electric blankets,
And flying suits for the RAF.

In a factory in Cheshire,
She was headhunted by NASA,
And promised the Congressional Medal,
For her work upon the treadle.

And they took her off windcheaters
On alternate afternoons,
To work full-time on space suits,
To take astronauts to the moon.

Everybody knows,
Neil Armstrong is the one
That matters most.
His suit was one of those
In which she sewed a secret stitch
The quality checker never found,
A lucky thread to keep him safe,
And both feet on the ground.
In the photographs you can see
The reassuring double tack
Stitched in the suit's left knee
Ensuring that he came back.

And Mrs. Armstrong softly said,
As they lay conjoined in terrestrial bed,
'Forget the dusty moon.
Tell me about the stars instead.'
And he recited four words of Wordsworth
He'd reserved for this occasion,
'Heaven lies about us,
No need to be a spaceman.'

And he blessed the secret seamstress,
Who, one flat Cheshire afternoon,
Tailored him a space suit
To fly home from the moon.

Hands

You put your left hand on mine, mine in yours.
A mirror of mine in hers, hers on mine.
It warmed my fingers, knuckles, palm and pores.
Two men together, with their hands entwined.

Held tight as you lay in your final bed,
By the hand that caressed and bowled the woods,
Made phone lines crackle into life from dead,
Rocked the cradle and pulled on boots.

That pinched out the snuff and passed round the port,
Flew Spitfires to safety with pilot's wings,
Mowed the Sports Club greens and the tennis courts.
A hand that could be turned to anything.

The same kind hand that gave your girl to me,
Will still hold mine, when you I cannot see.

Cycling City

Flat, tenfooted Hull, where I was born at home.
Such a little word for birthplace.
Not as tiny as Rye or Ely
But you must have saved me ink and space
And endless time, compared to someone born
In Schleswig-Holstein.

You welcomed me with a sea fret and a stench
Of fish, cattle cake and ashes from the blitz,
To a low land bevelled for bicycles,
Steered by lonely womanhood
Who ached for men at sea.

Dear departed Hull, in the care of Grandma Maud.
Raised my mother and her siblings
In the meanest lodgings.
Took me to a funeral for a treat, when I was eight,
In my gabardine mac with belt.

Sent me a hymn book for Christmas
Which she thought I'd like – marked,
'For Ken and those in peril on the sea',
And often said, mysteriously,
She'd seen 'Dr. Crippen on a bike'.

Dear dull, family history Hull. My nose stuck in
An estuary mud of books and verse,
Wrote some, flounders mostly, even worse.

My uncle knowing I admired the poets,
Told me he knew Larkin.
Transpired he only saw him cycling.
Neat, bespectacled, raincoated,
Thinking, hastening workward, like many then,
Unlike the flush trawler men,
Who drank deep and taxied, bloated,
Stinking, chastened, home again.

City of Culture Hull, jewel in the east,
Northern light over Dogger Bight.
Make the trawler nets bulge with
Poems full of tygers burning bright.

Cheer the nation,
Declare the River Hull as sacred,
And rename it with imagination,
Swop pier for Shakespeare,
Make Hull KR do ballet,
Change your name to Halle,
And swarm cycling city with pedalling poets,
Philip Larkin look-alikes, and
Doctor Crippens on their bikes.

Mondays

Wish I was there, where black swans dare,
And wildfowl roam, by Dawlish Water.
Not back at work, where Mondays lurk
Round every corner.

Washday drudge and dreary worry,
Sweat my way through in-tray slurry,
Bits and bobs, and awkward jobs,
I should have done on Friday.
Home to leftovers, cold potatoes,
Crusts of old pavlova.
No Smugglers Inn, or song and dance.
Early night and dim the light.
Getting friendly? Not a chance.

Wish I was there, where black swans dare,
And seabirds wheel in shallow flight,
No Monday morning feeling,
Before it's even light.
Wish I could roam towards Red Rocks,
Observing birds, not watching clocks.

Everyone Likes the Sound of Their Own Name

Kenneth Beevers is very tedious, but he's honest, upright, and abstemious. He definitely hasn't any previous, no spent convictions or restrictions, no teenage ASBOs or surrendered passports. He's so pristine and squeaky clean, he's a CRB checker's dream. No stains upon his copybook, no blots upon his jotter.

Kenneth Beever, eager beaver, has been spotted in the River Otter. Responds to stick and not the carrot but doesn't really like the race. He's like the canary my Aunt Mary noticed in the River Parrett, always somehow out of place. He's a Yorkshireman in Southern Devon, as boring as the River Severn.

Kenneth Beeve is softly spoken, quietly flowing like the Don. Often had his poor heart broken, now he wears it on his sleeve.

Kenneth Beev 'There are two of these. Go on, have one, take it please.' – he prefers to give than to receive.

Kenneth Bee is very busy, can be nimble and be quick, always working, never shirking, nails his colours to the mast, never has played loose and fast.

Kenneth Be or not to be, subject of soliloquy, thinks he's rather literary, writing silly poetry, very e-ponymously.

Kenneth B. Initially from Beverley.

Kenneth Connor and Kenneth Williams.
'Ooh Matron!' What a blooming *Carry On*.

Kennet canal that's linked with river Avon. Why does he just keep barging on and on? In a monotone without adventure, he sounds like a video in a garden centre.

Kenne Ball? Not that kind of man at all. Humility is his epithet, he never blows his own trumpet. He's not a genius like Dalglish – King Kenny's not his soubriquet!

Kenn Not a rake or Lothario, never mistaken for Ken Barlow. More Ken Dodd, the comic god, never knowing when to end ...

Ken is Barbie's special friend.

Ke? said the man from Barcelona.

K is a grand, lad, but his short life's over.

How to Make Yourself Disappear (Inspired by Simon Pitt)

Kenneth Beevers
Kenneth Beever
Kenneth Beeve
Kenneth Beev
Kenneth Bee
Kenneth Be
Kenneth B
Kenneth
Kennet
Kenne
Kenn
Ken
Ke
K
Ke
Ken
Kenn
Kenne
Kennet
Kenneth
Kenneth B
Kenneth Be
Kenneth Bee
Kenneth Beev
Kenneth Beeve
Kenneth Beever
Kenneth Beevers

Illumination

I have started a night class in creative writing
And find the homework quite exciting.
Setting, character or plot,
Dialogue, genre like as not,
I never know what's coming next,
In my tortured, laboured text.
I've mastered past and present tense,
And how to leave you …

In suspense.

I had a story up my sleeve,
And then without a by your leave,
Enter left Mahatma Gandhi –
I found the library rather handy.
When I told my brother on the phone,
I must have had a muffled tone.
'Creative Lighting! How does that work then?'
'You rack your brains and pick up pen,
And paper white as Bewick's swan,
And hope a little light comes on.'

Message

In the euphonious village of Doddiscombsleigh,
There is a glorious curiosity:
A green man with a cleft lip,
Fashioned by a mason's slip.
He is John Barleycorn, and Odin, Jack o' the Green,
And the May King, all aliases with many faces,
Disgorging fruit and hawthorn twigs.
Pagan men in ancient churches,
Hiding in their sacred places,
On misericords and wooden benches.
They whisper warnings from the vine,
Speak the wisdom of the leaves,
'Wake up, return to nature's ways.'

Rich Man in His Castle

We left the peaceful path at Berry Pomeroy,
And blundered into the shoot, like startled game,
Before their sorry reckoning.

The sky, once deathly pale, was pinking late,
And the wealthy guns were silent, unlike the noisy
Hired men, stood countrified and smoking at the gate.
Casually, one offered me a victim of the killing spree,
And I politely took it like a leaflet in the street.
An exchange of bird on string.
This made me ten years old again.

There was my father, in Harris Tweed, familiar
Smell of Old Spice, cigars and Swarfega,
Presenting me with a pheasant,
A gift from his employer.
Unsure, I took the loop, but surprised by the weight,
And shocked by its lifeless beauty,
I let it fall to ground once more.

That bird wasn't bred for sport or table.
Its secret flying mission was to sacrifice its plumage
For my mother's Women's Guild hat competition.

We watched its transformation, layered,
Glossy, almost breathing,
Not only would it win, it would surely fly again.
But there was no victory roll, or resurrection,
Just a mere commendation.

The hat was never worn,
But snugly stored in tissue,
Like a natural history specimen.

We ate our pheasant last night, pan fried quickly,
Swilled down with beer.
I relished each morsel, every scrap of memory,
That had slowly cooked for sixty years.

Bertie Lewis

You stopped the war, Bertie Lewis,
In Grosvenor Square, with love and peace,
Bertie Lewis, you were there.
You banned the bomb, Bertie Lewis,
In our town square, with your placard and petition,
Bertie Lewis, you were there.

You stand apart from blazered veterans,
On the margins of the crowd,
As you wait to lay your tribute to the fallen.
One more, this year – from the Falklands War.

Soon the memorial is bleeding with red wreaths,
Like cards resting on the mantelpiece,
Beneath the words no one ever reads,
Except you Bertie Lewis, man of peace:

'Our brothers died to win a better world.
Our part must be to strive for truth, goodwill, and peace,
That their self-sacrifice be not in vain.'

It is only forty yards to march and take the flak,
In your be-medalled leather coat and pork pie hat.
One for every bombing mission that you flew,
In the designated coffin space, of the gunner in the crew.
You were there, Bertie Lewis, you were there.

When someone paused,
You took your chance and walked,
And laid your wreath of poppies,
Pure as whitest chalk.

'We'll ban you', said the Legion, 'throw you out.
White poppies are not what wars are all about.'
But your offering stayed on the granite floor,

To stop the wars, stop the wars, end the tears.
Love and peace, Bertie Lewis, rest in peace.

For Hubert 'Bertie' Lewis 1920-2010
Born Chicago, Died Bolton

Poetry Island Discs

'And so, Ken, your first choice of music, please.'

The radio dial was the only light,
A pale green glow in the room I shared,
When I first heard,
On the Station of the Stars,
The electrifying opening bars
Of Dell Shannon singing *Runaway*.
Just after Chubby Checker and before Doris Day.

Suddenly, that narrow space
Was no longer dull or commonplace.
And I wondered ... would the morning show
How much I'd been changed by the radio?

And I still see our cast-iron beds.
Those remnants of Forth Bridge,
So sturdy and so angular,
They gave me bruises on my legs
But also served as desk and chair.
And sandwiched in between, a simple chest,
Clean pants, long socks and Aertex vests.
Below on the cold linoleum
Danced wispy balls of dust,
My brother said were bits of skin.

In that room we shared, I first heard,
On colourful Radio 208, a mesmerising poet say
That he was older yesterday.
Just after *Hang on Sloopy* and preceding *Wimoweh*.

And in that untidy space,
Everything fell into place:
My Dad was not the awkward one,
Just his now much younger son.
The poetry of *My Back Pages*,
I bought with my first wages.
And I wondered ...
Would my father see my musical epiphany?

And I still have my trinity,
Of book, watch and glass,
Next to the bed for sixty years.
Water from boards both north and south,
Has slaked my midnight thirst like needy tears.
A chain of nightly chapters,
As necessary as breathing,
Have led me to what I'm now reading,
While Timex, Dad's watch, and Casio,
Have marked the time I have to go.

In the house we shared, we often heard
On the Light Programme,
The treasured records of my Mum:
Edelweiss and *Release Me*,
Softly, as I Leave You.
I remember fondly,
Listening to *Family Favourites*,
Before our Sunday tea.

That tiny space became to me a hallowed place.
The background hum of my little life
Was the strings of Mantovani,
And Shirley Bassey's voice.
The only choice for many housewives,
As Long as He Needs Me.
And I wondered … would I ever leave
This home devoted to Jim Reeves?

So play for me *He'll Have to Go*,
And maybe once again I'll know,
The fire glow in our living room,
The needle on the gramophone,
The announcements from the foot of stairs,
As regular as calls to prayers:

'*Z Cars* is on.'

'YOUR TEA IS ON THE TABLE.'

'Kennedy's been shot.'
I jumped completely out of my skin
And hoped it was some hoax or trick.

'And so, Ken, your final choice of music.'

The radio dial gave the only light,
When I first heard, from Luxembourg,
The songbook steeped in loneliness,
The sound that only silence makes.
It was just after my nineteenth birthday,
The day I ran away from home.

Tattoos of Tenderness

I hold your hand,
Your slender wrist,
Sun spot kissed,
The fragile silk shelter of your skin
Stretched thin like a moth's wing
Over scar tissue,
On each side of your open palm,
Close to the soft
Whiteness of your inner arm.

Here were burns which never healed,
From self-harm every week
In battle with the oven, just for us.

Tattoos of tenderness,
Marks of a parent's love,
Now rarely seen,
Thanks to microwave and oven glove.

I Love Paris Road

Paignton is so à la mode,
Especially down by Paris Road,
Where à la carte and haute couture
Are absolutely de rigueur.
But if you walk along its pavements,
You won't find arrondissements,
Boulevards or Sacré-Cœur,
La Belle Époque or Gare du Nord.
You won't even find a bank
On Paris Road's unswept left flank.
Despite its continental air,
The whistle of chemin de fer,
That certain smell of Côte d'Azur,
And fish and chips, the plat du jour,
It only takes you to the pier,
'Kiss me quick', 'Wish you were here'.

No Piaf singing of regrets,
Just crows and seagulls, no egrets.
It's just a little out and back,
That yearns to be a cul-de-sac,
A dog leg round a bottle neck,
More cider sweet than demi-sec.
The raison d'être for this rue
Is a man called Paris Singer, who
Was born by happy chance,
In the capital of France.
So to both it does belong,
The Singer first and then the song.
This little road has such allure,
It sings for me Plaisir d'amour.

Why do I love this thoroughfare,
So nondescript beyond la mer?
I love it because she is there,
In our seaside pied-à-terre.

Just Desserts

Our seasons can't make up their mind.
They race ahead or lag behind,
Creep in slow and then fade out.
There always is some kind of doubt.
A winter glow, a summer cold,
Autumn crocus, Christmas rose.

The fabled fall can take its time,
And linger on serene, sublime.
Walk through Devon in this season.
It's all orchards, luscious Eden,
Juices flowing to excess,
To lubricate the cider press.

We passed a plank stretched over stones,
With bowls of Bramleys, garden grown,
And on a slice of cardboard box,
Illegible to hungry fox,
Some heart of gold had written **FREE**,
But we ignored this generous plea,
And left the apples overlooked,
Never to be oven cooked.

We like them red and so much sweeter,
So talked instead of English eater,
Mollie's Delicious and little Crispin,
Discovery and Orange Pippin.
And those whose teeth were not their own,
Spoke wistfully of sweet Braeburn.
Peasgood's Nonsuch and Golden Spire
Are apples that we all admire.
Chivers Delight and Crimson Queening
Are redolent with other meaning.
Norfolk Royal and Maiden's Blush
Provide the tangy sugar rush.
Byfleet Seedling is superb,
A crispy bite, a hint of herb.

And then the conference turned to pears,
And Devon apple cake and fairs.
This season gets its just desserts,
When autumn leaves, it almost hurts.

A Garden's Lament

Thirty years we loved each other,
But I was never yours, nor only yours, forever.
Long before your cultivation,
I had a past, revealed on municipal maps.

When you see a weeping willow,
Gracefully greening,
Or azalea flower in southern corner,
Weeks ahead of mine, in northern border,
Do not pine. I'm important now.
They pay a gardener, just to tidy me.

We have no binding ties.
He hasn't got your loving hands.
The pampered lawns still look down on me,
Think me shady, wild, dishevelled,
Not a proper plot, without a greenhouse,
And some seeds to pot.
She offers me tomatoes,
And says I give her nettles.

I still have my long, green lines,
Edged by lofty trees,
The reason why you wanted me,
And couldn't sleep until the deeds were signed.
I'm a playground once again,
Football pitch and cricket field,
Not a place of growth and yield.
You were a good custodian,
But we are only earth,
When all is said and done.

That Summer

We were skulking around Chudleigh Knighton,
On a bright, sunny morning in spring.
From the tangled limbs of the heathland,
A nightingale started to sing.
After years of summer impostors,
Rainswept, insipid, or fair,
It's song anticipated the heat wave
That soon would hang in the air.

As the shy, little scorcher emerged,
From this womb-like, sultry, soft spell,
The papers said that by August,
We'd all be roasting in hell.
The crops would wither and perish,
The economy crash in the strain,
Deeply deranged by temperature change,
And forty-five days without rain.

Working the fields of an Ipplepen farm
On a sensuous high summer night,
My white collar hands reaping the harvest,
Were bathed in a blood orange light.
At sunrise we slipped down to Meadfoot,
And entered the soothing cool sea.
There was no Brixham kipper,
Or homeward bound skipper,
As giddy that morning as me.

When feelings were heated, tempers were blazing
And we just couldn't sleep any more,
We drove out of Newton to Bovey,
And on to the shimmering moor.

We lay snake-still in the bracken,
In a cooling mesmeric trance,
Remembered a scene from *Gregory's Girl*,
And started the lying down dance.
The earth was lustre and biscuit,
The heather naturally swaled,

The night sky a roll of scorched parchment,
The starlight branded and Brailled.

Though these bouts of midsummer madness
Were slowly driving us wild,
Through all that dry barren season
We tried and we hoped for a child.
The secret stoked our desires,
And simmered in bedroom and stair
A longing unspoken, a yearning, a burning,
Like the heatwave that hung in the air.

His face was golden, like an icon,
And as lively as any King Sol.
He grew strong like the lion in winter,
But was fragile as any corn doll.
He's a man now, a husband, a father,
Warm-hearted, hot-blooded, and blessed
By a songbird's tranquil, soft calling,
And that summer's intense caress.

On the Warren

Observant, you love scanning the skies.
Free and flying, with your feet firmly on the ground.
Listening, in the din you pick them out,
Chiffchaffs, warblers, willow and wood.
An artist's eye. You spot them first,
Shouting. Not showing off,
Just seeing what I can't, when I merely look.
Grounded, you are lost to me when you are watching,
Or hunkered in our feathered bed, sleeping.
Murmuring, you are on the wing.
Endearing, your love of birds became a cause, a meaning,
A way of making sense, not just game or hobby.
Always you flying ahead, showing the way.

The John Charles Stamp

King John is pure Royal Mail.
His classic head and shoulders
Artfully fill the space,
With the handsome face of Wales.

A role model for the foot soldiers,
And the early rising sorts:
He's striking in red and immaculate in shorts.
He is a complete all-rounder:
Clever on the counter,
Knows where the posts are,
Pinpoint placement, top right corner.
Box to box traveller,
Defence unraveller,
With the timely delivery of the weighted pass.

Send him Par Avion,
He leaps like a salmon,
Flies like a bluebird to dominate the air.
This gentle giant handles parcels with care.
He's as happy abroad as he is at home,
On the green, green sward of Ninian Park.
He's only got one weakness:
He's impossible to mark.

And according to Stanley,
The official authority,
On football philately,
He is more valuable
Than the Hungarian triangle
Of 1953.

Man Lying on a Wall, 1957, By L. S. Lowry

He hangs on our half-landing, formally dressed,
As befits a clerk in the fifties.
Supine he lies, this man of some standing,
With a Woodbine clamped to his lips.
His head spins with prices
Of towelling and valances,
The checks and the balances
Of double entry ledgers and maths.
So, on his way home, he rests on a wall
At the back of the Crompton Street baths.

He's not shirking, he's working, and thinking,
And he definitely hasn't been drinking,
Unless it's a Friday or Tuesday,
When balancing just might be an issue.
Relaxed and insouciant,
And perfectly somnolent,
He favours a ventriloquist's dummy:
His large hands and face seem made out of wood.
He's a dozer, a napper, an afternoon kipper,
And, like me, he is misunderstood.

I make him talk when no one's at home.
I bring him to life and practise my skills
On the senior clerk at Haslingden Mills.

'Bottles of beer? I've only had one –
To get the mill out my throat.
I'm not really asleep,
I'm just thinking quite deep,
Sorting procedures for promissory notes.
I've worked out what's wrong with United:
They need a new forward line.
I'm worrying about our Susan's new boyfriend,
Hoping she comes home on time.

I'm deciding how to paper those tricky bits
That go round the dining room light,
And I'm frightened by the baby's bad coughing,
That only comes on in the night.
I'm wondering what the Prime Minister meant
By you've "never had it so good."
And if that's not enough,
Magic Moments is thread
Going round in my head.

I'm pondering the meaning of life.
It leaves no room for anything big.
I am a nobody, a clerk, just a man in the street
You'll not remember and, frankly, I don't give a fig.'

Then L. S. Lowry made him a saint,
To watch over men who can't stay awake.

Man Lying on a Wall, 2018,
By I. J. Beech

The Eternal Triangle

I fell in love with a girl who loved the moon, remote and cold,
The object of her affections four billion years old.
She loved me too, so I tried to shine,
Look pale and interesting and love her back,
As if she was only mine.

The moon showed her father the way,
As he flew back from wartime missions.
He called her Stella, and encouraged her ambitions.
She loved science – physics with its mysterious boxes
Of wires and connections, the instant drama of chemistry,
And best of all biology. It gave her a career in the laboratory,
A white coat I loved with its yellow chemical stains
And smells, and an image of cleverness and brains.

She talked to the moon and knew its phases better than mine,
But she said she loved me too, so I tried to shine,
Look pale and interesting and love her back,
As if she was only mine.

And then pieces of the moon came courting,
On a date at the Manchester Museum.
In a display of love they wooed her
And disturbed her equilibrium.
In front of her was not clinker
But a piece of flesh from the celestial body.
She was so moved her legs buckled
And she swooned as her eyes feasted on the basalt rock
Picked from The Sea of Tranquillity.

It was late when she got back
To her pungent coat of well washed white.
She didn't care because the girl had become
The girl who was in love with the moon,
And it was now her guiding light.

Yet still she said she loved me, so I tried to shine,
Look pale and interesting and love her back,
As if she was only mine.

We have spent the years lunar sightseeing on Dartmoor,
In the velvet black, watching snow moons, hare moons,
Harvest moons, wolf moons, blue moons and honeymoons,
Driving there in a Vauxhall Nova, then a Toyota Starlet,
And when that faded, a Ford Orion.
We chased eclipses and promised ourselves a Ford Galaxy.
In the darkness and quiet, I marvelled at the beauty,
And the aptness of her name.

The only worry I ever had was time
But she always said, 'Time does not flow, it just is',
And it has brought me to this moment,
When all I can do is try to shine,
Look pale and interesting and love her back,
As if she was only mine.

White Dress

In her crow's-nest bedroom,
She slept so close to the sea
It pervaded her dreams
And she grew to be like it:
Mercurial, naturally lovely and deep.
Content once to wash away footprints
And re-arrange pebbles,
The sea smashed railway line, seawall,
And roared at the windows.

Rescued at dawn, she abandoned her train
And the dress of organza, wrapped up in dreams.
In borrowed gown, her blue-sea eyes shining,
She waltzed around the guests.

Exposed by the wind,
The lonely outfit
Danced on its hanger
Like a white marionette.

The Battle of Spittle Street

I am not any old jug. I am Dartington blown glass. Lorna, the Parish Clerk, insisted on it, choosing me carefully. She said I would look the business in the little room of the village hall that they grandiosely call the Council Chamber. And I would help with decision making, which was not the councillors' strong point. 'What', she argued, 'could be more appropriate in our Devon village, than water served in a crystal jug, handcrafted in our own county?' She got her way but had to wait for the next year's budget to buy the matching glasses. Though I say so myself, we do look smart and important and we make a great team, in contrast to the elected members.

Council matters are often tedious but sometimes a subject will ignite the room and no amount of water can quench the flames of controversy. Moving a lamp-post once caused a crisis, and a minor heart attack, but nothing will ever match the legendary 'Battle of Spittle Street'. This led to seven extraordinary general meetings, two resignations and some minor fisticuffs. I had never been so busy. The meetings went on into the night and I was filled again and again. When the quarterly bill came, Lorna asked for the meter to be checked, and then had to ask for a supplementary rate to pay the bill.

This is what happened. Ten years before, Mr. and Mrs. S. retired to the village from the northern wastes up country, purchasing a spacious thatched house in the aforementioned street, a byway of wealth and beauty which belied its name. Their address was 2 Spittle Street. As time went on, they added an extension and converted a barn for guests. Others in this privileged enclave followed suit and they began to get increasingly unhappy with their address and its connotations.

Mr. S. went to see our chairman, Councillor Templecombe, in the tap room of the Church House Inn, where he received drinks and constituents at his official Friday night surgeries, as he ostentatiously called them. Mr. S. told him they were not best pleased to say where they lived: the name was vulgar and made them feel ashamed. It was, he said, not a suitable name for a street in which all the properties were in the highest council tax band in the county, and it was giving his wife a complex. They deserved better. There was evidence that in the distant past the name of the street was Manor Road. It should be investigated and, if proven, restored. The Chairman asked them to put their request in writing.

Lorna referred to them as newcomers when she read their letter out at the next council meeting. Templecombe was contemptuous. He said, 'As far as I know, it was called Spittle Street in the Domesday Book. They can move if they don't like it.' There was little discussion and Lorna was asked to write back.

Mr. S. did not give up. He got some support from his friends in the golf club, the gastro pub with its Michelin Bib and his neighbours in their soft yellow-stoned mansions. He got more backing from the estate agent, who said the properties would rise in value if the road had, just as an example, a name associated with grander things, such as the old Manor House that used to be up the hill. Mr. S. sent in a small petition on the finest Basildon Bond paper.

Shortly after that, the County Council got involved, by nature of Mr. S.'s contacts in high places. They wrote to say they had done some mapping checks and it transpired that Spittle Street might have been wrongly named in the past and could be the tiny unnamed track adjacent to it. Our leader banged the table so hard, I wobbled a bit. 'It is time to get the big guns in', he said. And he contacted the Local History Society's secretary, who had once been on *Who Do You Think You Are?*

She knew her stuff and the society was one of the best in the area. However, unfortunately, they had never successfully proved the origin of this intriguing but down to earth name. Old Rosemary said that it was because the fields there were always covered in cuckoo spit. The Society endorsed the fact that the name should not be changed and threw its considerable force of seven members, including Old Rosemary, one hundred village-related artefacts and forty hours of tape-recorded dialect, behind the cause. In the best tradition of criminal detection, they worked round the clock listening to the tapes, in case any reference to Spittle Street had been missed when they were transcribed.

Meanwhile, the Anti-Spittle Street group engaged a barrister and a slippery negotiator 'well versed in using documents to prove anything you like', or so our leader said.

Lorna collected other evidence from interested parties. A spokesperson for the Post Office said, 'It was always Spittle

Street as far as we're concerned but the modern service can adapt to anything, as we use postcodes for established reference points.' She added that on this subject, Human Resources had interviewed old Jim Easterbrook, who had been the postie for the villages around Newton Abbot for over forty years and was the world expert on their lanes, tracks, paths and etymology. He said it was universally known as 'Up Theer' when he first started. Before the big new houses and amazing cottage conversions, it was also known as 'Top of the Cabbage Field' but it was still always Spittle Street – like the poem.

The fact that it featured in a poem by a famous poet was very important. It was in print, in published works, in anthologies, studied for GCSE, it was sacrosanct. Lorna thought that would be the end of it. It could never be changed and the council asked her to write citing this as evidence.

By now the row had gone public and villagers began to take sides. Mr. S. wrote back an emotional letter, saying people had called his wife 'gobby' and he wasn't having it. He demanded a public meeting. Councillor Smallcombe, a fence-sitter and an opportunist if ever there was one, agreed.

It was put to the vote, and a meeting was arranged. The village hall was full and so was the car park, where the proceedings were relayed by loudspeakers. There were two camps: New Money versus Birthright. One villager said, 'Why don't they just call it Mayfair and have done?' The idea was 'as mazed as a wheelbarrow'. The outcome was a referendum, in the name of democracy. Lorna had to get supplementary funds from the County to pay for it.

There was just one question on the form distributed to every resident: Should the name of Spittle Street be changed? Yes or no?

The result was in the balance but it was then that our Chairman came up with his master stroke – a power sharing agreement with the village hall subcommittee. He did a deal behind closed doors with Elsie Luccombe and the influential group who ran the village hall, the real power in the village. In return for a new Burco boiler, and a dozen tea towels, they promised to give all their support to the Keep Spittle Street Campaign, and to lobby all the villagers they could to vote for the status quo. It was a done deal and it worked.

Elsie's team distributed to every household a flyer with the poem on it. The vote was overwhelmingly for common sense and tradition and Spittle Street was preserved.

Sipping water, poured from me, her favourite jug, the Parish Clerk took great satisfaction in confirming the decision in writing.

Dear Mr. and Mrs. Sidebottom ... she began.

The Date

It was a winter morning in 1937 and Samuel, my older brother, had got up early for his Saturday morning stint at the mill. He was going on his first date after work and had already confided to Mum that he was in love. Mum, who was a real good sort, had been the first person down our steep little stairs that morning and, because of the excitement, I'd given up my lie in as well to see him off. Since Dad died, we had done things together.

Mum was worried because our house was due to be demolished and we didn't know where we would be living. All around our street, the wrecking gangs had been at work and there was a permanent stench of slum bricks in the air. Mum said she didn't want to move from 'the sunniest spot in Bolton' but I knew it was because there were so many memories there.

We didn't have electricity, only gas, and that week the gas mantle in the kitchen had gone. It was never replaced straight away, because it was a fiddly job and we couldn't always afford a new one. It was a habit to go without because when Dad was alive, he never let us put the light on until we were walking into the furniture.

The night before, Samuel had taken a bowl of hot water into the front room and shaved, then trimmed his moustache, and a great palaver was made of that. He then parcelled a change of clothes to wear after work, when he was taking Edith, from the mill offices, to the matinee at the Hippodrome. Our Samuel didn't keep his thoughts to himself and all week he had looked forward to the date as if it was the nearest thing to heaven he could imagine. It was pitch black in the kitchen that morning and paradise seemed far away as Samuel stripped to the waist for his wash. He'd done this many times before in the dark and knew exactly where everything was.

Mum and I sat in the front room, where she had already lit the fire and the gas light. Apart from the reassuring sound of the light, all we could hear was Samuel going about his ablutions. The noise of water splashing, the tap running and the slapping of flesh sounded more like a walrus at play than a working man beautifying himself. Every so often there would be a lull and then the whole business would start again until it sounded like several walruses and a hippopotamus thrown in for good measure.

Eventually there was silence, replaced by the little noises, such as the odd curse, that indicate a man is putting on the rest of his clothes and getting his things together in a bit of a panic, as he is late for work. Samuel, ready at last, came in to say goodbye and get his sandwiches from Mum.

'Good luck, son', she said, 'and enjoy yourself.'

'I will, Mum.' As he opened the door to go, he added, 'Oh Mum, don't buy any more of that new soap. It's useless. I couldn't get any sort of lather with it. Go back to Leverhulme's best.'

The door slammed and he was gone. Mum looked puzzled.

'What is he talking about? I haven't bought any new soap. Billy, go in the kitchen and bring the soap in here.'

I got up and went into the dark kitchen, located the soap and saucer and brought them into the front room. Straight away I saw Samuel's big mistake and went weak at the knees. Mum just screamed. On the saucer was a dead mouse, soaking wet and showing signs of some very rough treatment, a consequence of going six rounds with Samuel's hairy armpits.

'That poor boy. That poor, poor boy', she said, and the tears began to flow down her cheeks. She put her head in her hands and sobbed, her chest heaving with sadness.

I gently put my hand in hers and whispered, 'Never mind, Mum.'

She looked up and I realised she was laughing. When she saw the moribund mouse that had been mistaken for a slab of Sunlight, the laughter was uncontrollable. Her whole body was shaking and I couldn't help but join in.

'However will we tell him?' she said.

While we considered this, I had a thought. 'I'll tell you what, Mum. He'll enjoy them cheese sandwiches today', and that set us off again.

As the time came for Samuel to come home, Mum got quieter and quieter but she needn't have worried. Samuel was talking as soon as he opened the door, about how well it had gone and how special Edith was. I noticed that Mum could not look him in the eye, in case she laughed.

'She's not like the other girls at work, Mum, always gossiping and talking about each other. She's not a bit ..., what's the word? ... '

'Catty?' said Mum.

'Yes, that's it.'

'I reckon that's just as well', she laughed and could not contain herself any longer.

'What's so funny?'

'Son, sit down. I've got something to tell you. You must be strong. In fact, when I've told you about this little misfortune, how you take it will determine whether you are a man or a m....', and with that she became helpless with laughter again.

The first thing he did next day was to go to Skinner's corner shop and buy some candles. He never washed in the dark again, and Edith asked him to shave off his whiskers.

Bullsh*t

From the *Evening News*, April 2001
Wealthy people are choosing our town as the place they want to live. According to a survey, it is the new playground of the rich. The leader of the council said it reflects the efforts the council has made.

From the *Evening News*, April 2001
In another survey, the quality of life in our town was today branded one of the worst in the country. The leader of the council described the report as meaningless and totally unscientific.

The definition is terminological inexactitude.
That's bullsh*t for falsehood and meaningless platitude.
If you can speak it or write it, you are an artist.
It's simpler to join in than it is to resist

Because Bullsh*t is the new Esperanto:
It's a universal language, not just banter or political panto.

It wins every argument.
It's in all advertisements.
It's the millennium bug, an adulterer's hug.
It tastes like horse meat lasagne.
It's a straight crooked line,
The thief of our time,
Tautology, kidology,
A government apology
Invented by bullsh*t departments.

It's the closing down sale
And all of the lyrics
Of *A Whiter Shade of Pale*.

So let rip the trite fandango,
Bullsh*t is the new Esperanto.
If you can speak it or write it, you are an artist.
It's simpler to join in than it is to resist.

Papers were tigers once,
Comment was free
And all of the facts were sacred.
Now they recycle ignorance,
Write what they're fed
On a plate with a nice sprig of parsley.
The only 'true facts'
Grace a packet of fags.

Bullsh*t is the new Esperanto.
It feeds all the deals
And greases the wheels.
We don't know whether we stand
On our heads or our heels.
If you can speak it or write it, you are an artist.
It's simpler to join in than it is to resist.

Tomorrow is National Wash Your Hands Day,
Saturday is National Croissant Day.
*And every day is Bullsh*t Day.*

Rogue's Treasures

Every night, from mesonoxian silence
To birdsong of dawn chorus,
I sleep with a thesaurus.

There is no pillow talk
Spent in pleasant review of the day,
Or planning the next,
Only stray prompts of insomnia,
Harsh, uninvited, vexed.
Accusations, minor sins,
A fathomless sea of imaginings,

Until a different light reveals
Thirty phrases for morning,
And oceans of words to live for,
From cock crow to midnight quiet.
What a rogue, what a life, full of treasures.

The Old School Ties

My new school died when it was young,
Of cancer in the concrete,
School ties already threadbare.
The day it opened, uniformed and neat,
There were no famous alumni
Or walls clad in ivy, just High Alumina Cement.
No need to mourn: it was no James Dean,
Just ugly, fifties, with a mezzanine.
There'll be no reunion on its parquet floors,
Where I once stood in hushed assembly
And listened to a eulogy,
For someone who died young,
His name a stumble on my tongue.
A man who died for decency,
So at least decency survived.
Peacemaker, poet, statesman,
Secretary General of the United Nations,
A hero of our time,
I embraced as one of mine.

And the bell tolled for dinner time …
And Dag Hammarskjöld.

Even the food was an education.
We dined in a refectory.
I told my mum we had ragout,
And the roast potatoes
Were the best I'd ever tasted.
'They've got big ovens', she said.
'I've only got a little Creda.
Don't forget your roots.
Don't get too big for your boots.
Ragout's only Irish stew.'
Another lesson learned.

And the bell tolled for lessons …
And Dag Hammarskjöld.

Cauliflower au gratin
Set us up for double Latin.
Mr Davies, leaning on an empty desk,
Gazed upon us circumspect.
A giant bat in a gown of black,
He couldn't miss the pinned-up page,
A picture of Kim Novak,
With very little on her back.

'Pin-ups fade', he said,
'When their star no longer shines.'
And he gave us the lesson of our lives,
On self-respect and feminism,
The beauty and grace of men and women,
The joys that physical love can bring,
Equally taken, equally given.
And we must strive for decency,
So decency survives.
And the light burned in his eyes,
As he taught us to be civilised.

My pin-up was Duncan Edwards
With number 6 upon his back,
A hero of our time,
I embraced as one of mine.

'Just a tin god in football boots, lad', he said.

And the bell tolled …
For Duncan Edwards
And Dag Hammarskjöld.

John Brodie Lived Here

I have an addiction. It's only mild;
It won't hurt an unborn child.
It's not alcohol or crack –
I just like to read blue plaques.
Badges on a building's lapel
Can never lead you into hell –
But they can make you a bore.
Did you know Queen Victoria has forty? –
And John Wesley has three more?

In my running days,
I was always at the back.
In the London Marathon,
I read all nine hundred plaques.
For The Liverpool Half,
I was determined not to stop,
But according to the *Liverpool Echo,
Liverpool Echo*,
There were several plaques each mile,
And each mile was a Beatles song.
A flying start, *It Won't Be Long*.
Parliament Street, *Let It Be*.
Toxteth Cemetery, *Eleanor Rigby*.
At *Love Me Do*,
A flash of blue,
Led me up a garden path
And told me
That John Brodie,
City Engineer,
Lived here.

Do You Want to Know a Secret?
He designed the Mersey Tunnel –
And invented the football net.

I stood in reverence and attention,
Heard swish of ball,
Saw balletic ripple of goals
Too numerous to mention.
If I had died,
At 28 Ullet Road,
Breathed my last breath
And lost my soul,
My cause of death would have been
Own goal.

The Lost Art of Goalpost Chalking

The casual betrayal of childhood,
NO BALL GAMES BY ORDER,
Made us enemies of the estate, and criminals at eight,
For loving the sound of the rebound
And the mortared mystique of soccer in the street.
Contemptuous of sports fields with bourgeois nets and stanchions,
The chalky-fingered architects of football's ancient grounds
Carried on as outlaws, avant-garde and lawless,
Never to be scoreless. On any brickwork canvas,
Where gable ends stood idle, unemployed on corners,
They drew goalposts to be shot at by anarchic centre forwards.
Right to left, sequential, in ritualistic lines,
Incorporating drainpipes and corporation signs,
Like Dadaesque surrealists in revolutionary times.

Planet Earth Diary

3 May Dear Jim, Forgive me, the memories were just too hard to bear. I've sold the house and moved to senior living, without the only life that matters. I feel like I have left you. You would love it here: peeps of sea, spitting distance of Morrisons and a grandstand view into the zoo. I hope I make friends. No one was in the communal room but down below the orangutans were having a friendly conflab. They are good neighbours. Give me great apes any day. This is my new address. I need to know I've told you. I'm in the same familiar bed, with the happy memory mattress. Feeling close to you, Edith

4 May Dear Jim, Exotic noises woke me. I dreamt we were intertwined trees lying in the rainforest. You are still with me, like the imprints of the vines on the brick glaze of my body. To relieve pain, there is bingo and the company of other widows, and singing. The orangutans are friendly but here we are all strangers. I cried tonight. I have bought a yearly pass for the zoo and anytime I feel lonely I am going to have a chat with the orangutans. They've got endearing habits. They remind me of you, Jungle Jim. Love, E

5 June Dear Jim, There was a hell of a din this morning at 5a.m. I looked out and there was a Roman orgy going on in the ape house. I shut the curtains and listened to Farming Today. Olive and the card school have fallen out with me. All they do is watch soaps and play cards. The apes were still at it later on. Late Spring Fever, I suppose. The art of grieving is keeping busy, so I watched and wrote it all down, in detail, just like David Attenborough. We weren't meant to be on our own, Jim. I feel like I am in a cage. If I was a red panda, someone would be scouring the world's zoos for a mate for me. Not that I want one. You were the only one for me. Love you forever, E

5 December Dear Jim, It's not been a good day for getting on with the inmates. We could learn from the animals, who rub along nicely together. Remember that Grace I told you about, the one next door? She is off my Christmas card list. She banged on the wall when I put Aled Jones on tonight. I call her the Warrior Queen of the Jungle. Also, Betty said to me today, rather pointedly, 'It's a pity you've got no family, Edith.' She gets visitors all the time. When I used to tell people we weren't blessed with children, they would say to me 'But you've got Jim.' Not your fault you left, God rest your soul. You are only in my Tarzan dreams now. You were my mate for life, but you forgot the script. Last night I dreamt I was sitting on one of those memorial benches, with flowers on, permanently clinging to the past. I don't want to be a lonely old widow. I celebrate our life but this is a new one. Missing your goodnight kiss, Edith

25 January Dear Jim, The warden organised a Burns Night supper. Feeding time was at 6p.m. Haggis, neeps, tatties, whisky, and a clotted cream tea. I tried to make conversation. Afterwards, they all went in the TV room to watch *Big Brother*. There were anguished noises from the zoo tonight. I recognised a gibbon. It sounded like Roy Orbison singing *Only the Lonely*. I laughed but then I cried, and got angry with you for leaving me. Maybe I shouldn't have moved. Rest In Peace, Tarzan.

1 February Dear Jim, There is a monkey always looking up at me. He's an outsider. The others don't let him join in. He doesn't mix and just watches my window. I think he is a kindred spirit. There was a talk by a zoo keeper, who was very interested in my zoo diary. What do you think of that, Jim? I'd rather be observing your comings and goings though: the way you read the paper, always folding and smoothing it, your explosive nose blows first thing in the morning, so loud they rattled the walls, the innocent way you enquired if we were having wine with our tea. I miss you talking to the television, telling the BBC they've got a bloody cheek. What's that word – idiosyncrasies? You had plenty of them and I miss them all. To celebrate a special day, I had a glass of wine tonight. I had your glass as well but I missed your company. Love and cheers, Edith

8 February Dear Jim, I went to the Friends and Volunteers meeting at the zoo. I read some of my observations from my zoo diary. I made friends. Every Tuesday is Friends Day. They might find me a job! The warden organised a Chinese New

Year Party. There was crispy duck and a clotted cream tea. I shall go to the zoo tomorrow and wish the monkey a Happy Chinese Year of the Monkey. The animals were quiet tonight, all longing to be somewhere else. In the silence, I heard you say, as I switched on the light, 'That's another lantern of loneliness glowing dim above the bay.' E

14 February Dear Jim, I think the monkey likes the cut of my jib. Did you know you were a monkey, born 1944? He looked at me like you used to. Trying to work out my mood, weigh me up. 'What have you got planned for me now?' sort of thing. That querulous look you had when you said 'Am I allowed a bit of cake with my afternoon tea?' or 'How about an afternoon nap?' The warden organised a Valentine's Day social. We had a heart-throb themed cream tea. Howard from Flat 10 says he is going to complain to social services if he is forced to eat any more clotted cream. I might do a class in animal psychology but don't worry, Jim – I'd still rather study you.
Your Number One Fan, Edith

P.S. When you want to haunt me next, please remember my new address. I'm in the same familiar bed with the happy memory mattress.

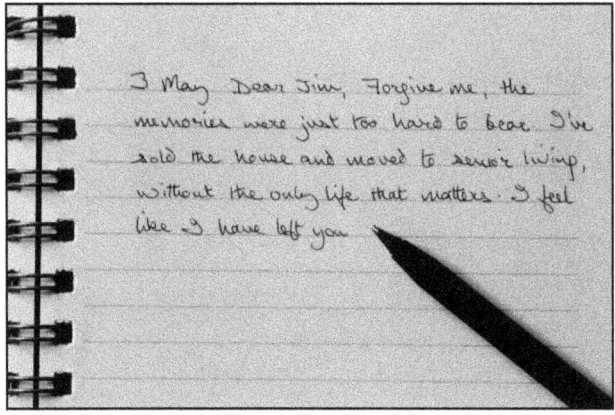

The Rose Bowl

The silver rose bowl sits on our sideboard,
An heirloom my mother would not give houseroom,
Though when her father won it,
Thousands cheered his last lap home.

It's back on parade,
But cross-examined will only reveal
Its hallmark, serial number, and name.
Won by John Noyland, first local man,
1913 Hull Marathon.

It sits on a shabby pedestal
My mother never put him on.
Looks like my flesh and blood:
Familiar round face, shiny cheeks.
The mesh heart is missing,
The surface tarnished.

Once it held red roses for courtship,
White for marriage,
But somewhere in Picardy
The grandad I never knew
Was changed by the stew of war,
Lost the fingers on his wedding hand,
When black roses signalled
Death and farewell to a brother in arms.

The yellow roses for welcome back
Soon smelt of decay.
There was no work for the local hero
And no prizes for a father
Who ran away from home.
He was not the first this time.

I buy some blooms to forgive the sorry soldier,
But put them in a vase
And fill the bowl to the brim with fruit.
My mother was always hungry.

The Clotted Cream Diaries

Far from our familiar home,
A blizzard of cards awaited us.
'Farewell old friend', they said, 'remember me,
And please send clotted cream regularly,
Packed in tins, and paper-wrapped,
Boxed and tied with parcel string,
Adorned with different-coloured stamps,
Redolent of holidays,
And God's West Country railways.'

I scoured the soured streets
Of once bejewelled towns,
Below milk white villas
And soft-hued seaside flats,
Looked on shelves and in wire bins
Of community-minded village inns
But shops which once dispatched dreams
Were now enriching charities.

Dairy Hill led only to an overspill
Of cream-skimmed quart pot semis.
The relics of the creameries
Stood like tin mine chimneys
And east and west of river Exe,
The bakeries were gone,
With their different names for scone:
The tuffs, and splits, and chudleighs
Were madeleines of memories.

Now, Devon is an ancient land.
In a county town museum,
There's a farmhouse full of artefacts:
Trivets, tongs and roasting jacks,
Salamanders, spits and skewers.
Alongside entrenched attitudes,
Where men must work the plough,
And women tend the cow,
With everything for making cream:
Skimmers, muslin, scalding pans,
Butter tubs, and clever hands.

An inglenook,
The sound of clocks,
A chair beside the fireplace,
And resting on the mantelpiece,
A postcard from the battlefields.
'Mother, I am on the mend,
Remember me to all kind friends.
Give my regards to Buckfastleigh
And please send clotted cream regularly.'

The Greatest Shakespearean

I saw him, the greatest ever Shakespearean,
One dull afternoon, transcend everything,
Surpass Olivier, Richard Burton,
Dench's Ophelia and Sir Henry Irving.

Listen ... It was way back in the 1960s
On a school trip marred by bad behaviour.
He graced the matinee with genius:
Oh, man, you should have seen his cool King Lear.

But the class prat smote him with a pellet
From his bag of childish slings and arrows.
Stately calm, he acted the professional,
Blind to cocky culprit in the shadows.

At curtain call, he blocked our crocodile,
Said, 'Soft you, a word or two before you go.'
His gaze alighted on the philistine,
His eloquence was masterful and slow.
Said he, 'When I do stare, see how the subject quakes,
You whining schoolboy, with a satchel,
Mildewed ear, thou cream-faced loon, fat as cakes.
You are not worth the dust
Which the rude wind blows in your face.
You are got by the devil himself.
Out you bloody fool
And rot in hell
Your dismal codpiece of a grammar school.'

Forsooth, I tell you in this aside ...

Quite soon our school, proud and new and built to last,
Subsided, disappeared almost overnight,
Recipient of his Macbeth's cursed blast,
And pestilential concrete blight.
And that was the great John Neville's last word upon it,
No ifs or maybes,
We were all banned from Nottingham Playhouse,
From then, for ever, *sine die*.

The Light of the World

More famous in our town
Than its celebrities
Or self-seeking mayor,
Was a nameless recycler,
Living on nothing
But plates of thin air.
A tramp with a trolley,
And an impossible load,
Who slowed down the traffic
On the Manchester Road.

Regally-bearded,
Some said he was royalty,
The Times crossword setter,
A shy millionaire,
Left at the altar,
Driven by despair
To pick up the pieces
On the Manchester Road.

He spent Christmas Eve scrounging,
On the Old Market ground,
Found an abandoned road lantern,
An old wooden post,
Pieces of chicken
And Norwegian spruce,
Then circled the darkness
In a well-practised loop,
For the sweepings and leavings,
For vegetable soup,
To banish the cold
On the Manchester Road.

Then I nearly killed him
As I rounded the bend,
Where the fog from the Irwell
Met the light of the world.
Huge overcoat flapping
On the frame of a ghost,

The lantern was hanging
From the end of the post.
The supermarket trolley
Blazed like a star,
Enshrined in the light
That shone from the car,
Beatific features
Upturned to the sky,
The salvaging saint
Had joined the magi,
Recycling gold
On the Manchester Road.

The Blow-In

Call me blow-in, call me drifter,
Walk on part, scenery shifter,
Afghan kite, Chinese light,
Traffickers' wheels in dead of night.
Capricious, moving, weather vane,
I don't even have a name.
I am the leaves that gather in piles,
I am feathers, I am chimes,
Windblown answer for these times.
Call me spots of Saharan sand,
You can never hold my hand.
Call me short let, not a very good bet,
Call me problem, call me threat,
Displaced person, refugee,
Smuggled survivor, adrift at sea.
Call me desperate and reviled,
Asylum-seeking, terror-fleeing,
Call me child and human being.
Call me blow-in, call me drifter,
Walk on part, scenery shifter.

Walking the St. Swithun's Way, July 2012

At the start, a man in huge, worn-out boots
Told us to 'Beware of snakes in the grass.'
So, warily we followed the shell-marked route,
Out of Surrey's flinty fields,
Through crops of barley, potatoes, broad beans,
Into Hampshire's old hop country,
Past pubs even a saint couldn't walk by,
To reach Alton, along a road
Carved out of ancient woodland,
And a honeymoon of a night.

A man who drove a steam train told us,
'You'll never grow old
If you do something you love.'
The path began to twist and turn,
Unlike his permanent way, and in the rain,
We argued and lost direction,
Sang her old school song, *To Be a Pilgrim*,
And were hopeful, not discouraged,
Reaching Jane Austen's House at Chawton,
Where the trail in her name
Persuasively pointed the way.

A woman who loved working there told us,
'You'll need more than sense and sensibility
To keep you on track.'
So, laughing, we threw away the map,
Walked past watercress beds,
Along the River Itchen and its streams,
Chalky things of beauty,
Thick with marbled whites
And demoiselle damselflies.
We sang and shouted *Ruby, Ruby, Ruby*
But singer of the walk was the yellowhammer,
Constant in the stillness and the solitude.

There was no sign of rain, or other pilgrims,
But at Headbourne Worthy's tiny church in his name,
The Friends of the Saint, celebrating his day,
Gave us tea and told us to 'Stay friends.'

It started with a short walk up the aisle on St. Swithun's Day.
When we reached Winchester Cathedral and the shrine,
We had walked forty miles, and been married forty years, exactly,
Rain and shine.

Priceless

I have nothing to take
To the *Antiques Roadshow*.
No Ming vases used as doorstops,
Jilted royal lover's locket
Or a year's wages' worth of jewellery
Discarded in a drawer.
Just reminders from my mother's house:
Tiepin, cuff links,
An ashtray with *Jersey* written on it.

And my father's jam jars,
Full of Rawlplugs, washers, nuts,
Replenished
Like lifeblood.
Bequeathed from his shed to mine,
In a tradition
Handed down
And perfected over time.

When I empty contents on to newspaper,
There's no need to rummage through
The disordered metal stew.
Shining, like his spirit, will be the required screw.

I Was Reading

What was that? I'm sorry, Dad.
I didn't hear you, I was reading.
I was boosting my vocabulary,
Chewing on a particularly delicious word,
Like a succulent piece of salami.
The word was vicariously,
Your favourite word for me.
You know, living in my imagination,
There's no limit on words.
You can have as many units as you want.
No need to fast. I am ravenous.
I am a bookaneer.

I am learning from the voices of the past.
It's giving me a sex education,
The one that you and school forgot.
I am learning about its strange realities,
In fiction, not the *Reader's Digest*.
Have you had the complaint, Dad?
The one like Portnoy?

Have you read it?
Made me feel normal
But made me feel faint.
If a femme fatale comes along,
I want to know how to recognise one.
And I'm keeping my options open,
In case I meet a Don Juan,
With Byronic good looks.
I need to prepare for
The End of the Affair.

Have you read it, dad?
Can you love someone that much?
I'm still recovering.
Better keep an eye on me.
I've not been the same since
The Grapes of Wrath crossed my path.
I want to know how to talk,

And listen. I don't want to fumble,
I want to know how to touch.

What did you say?
I'll be with you in a minute.
Just one more page.
I am somewhere else,
Not in this country town;
I am *On the Road*.

Have you read it, Dad?
Sex, drugs, nomadic wanderlust,
And Jack Kerouac chopping down
Telegraph poles with an imaginary axe,
As he travelled Route 66.
I used to do that, Dad,
So I must be normal.
I must be soulful.

I am escaping
With my book.
Whoever it's by,
It's always mine.
We are comrades.
It welcomes me back
With its fragrant smell,
Like an old dog.

It's making me discontented,
In a good way.
My pulse rate's up.
It's like watching the Wanderers;
I am being saved.
I am becoming interesting and attractive,
And curious.
I am a detective.
I am broke
But I am rich,
Because I am reading,
Without prejudice.
I have empathy,
Because reading taught me.

Sorry I disturbed you last night
With my laughing,
And the light.
I have to read,
In the stillness of near midnight,
To ease the unbearable longing
And restlessness of this human heart.
The Heart is a Lonely Hunter –
And reading is a twenty-four hour job.

By the way, Dad.
My mates say you're Dickensian.
Now I know why –
Because I've been reading.
He was a genius, by the way.

Bonjour Tristesse

Françoise Sagan,
Your name was a poem on my tongue.
I read your novels one by one,
When I was young, impressionable.
Slim volumes in my blazer pocket
Made me feel sophisticated,
Each title succinct,
A work of art in Penguin ink.
Bonjour Tristesse.
A better phrase for being fed up,
That side effect of growing up,
A book of free love, and glamour,
The long-legged Cécile,
And the permissive society, which passed me by,
Did not apply in our suburban semi.
Mistresses were unknown in our road.
When Cécile took hot coffee and an orange for breakfast,
And went out into the delicious Riviera morning,
That was a revelation without warning.
For I had never had anything but shredded wheat
And mug of tea, in a cold kitchen, in a cold English street.

I used to do local history talks. One night I was double booked with a rat catcher from Oldham. They had a vote on it. I lost. I went home and told my wife I was going to be a performance poet instead. These were her very words …

Don't Get Mad, Get Even

Don't get mad, get even.
Change direction like that cool Cat Stevens,
Say farewell to the history, boy,
And scribble me some odes to joy.
Step outside your dreary shoes,
Drive me wild, make me your muse.
Oh, you remind me of Ted Hughes.
There's a Scouser in you somewhere –
You could be a millionaire.
Remember William Butler Yeats,
Nothing comes to he who waits.
Be Hiawatha, not Chief Librarian,
Louis MacNeice, not my antiquarian.

Don't be second-bested,
Poetry is hairy-chested.
You really are so Gerald Manley,
Braver than young Laurie Lee –
And he was a real tough trucker.
You can swear like Cooper Clarke.
It would stop me dozing in the dark
And, compared to him, you're quite a looker.
You could be the new Lord Byron,
Reciting *Albert and the Lion*.

Once you've whetted my appetite,
Do not go gentle into that good night.
Overwhelm me with desire,
Leave me feeling I'm on fire.

Then take me hunting for the snark.
It's incumbent on you
To show me what a bit of Larkin leads to.

Shirt Tale

Once a scarf was enough, worn with wariness.
Now only a shirt will do, worn with pride.
There are thousands of us, properly dressed,
And half a city more in devil's red
Across the green divide.

We roar with equal belief at the first skirmishes,
Flushing a bat from its roost in the old Wembley rafters.
Made in Bangladesh of artificial threads,
Our tops are soft and smooth as rabbit's fur,
Unlike the one I used to wear on Saturday afternoons,
When I played for the Stapleford Methodists
Against other Sunday Schools.

We undressed behind the hedgerows,
Warmed our legs with liniment,
And shivered into knickers,
Put on long white stockings
And threadbare worn-out jerseys,
In the colours of the Gunners.
When football was innocent,
These were the terms for kit.
From First Division to Isthmian League,
It was in the programme notes.

Ashamed of my temperance outfit,
My mother used her sewing basket
Of remnants, bits and bobs
To invent club colours for supporters,
The money-spinner of the Gods.

The twentieth century icon,
The first replica football shirt,
Was ready by the morning,
And hanging with the ironing,
On our front room architrave,
Already itching to kick,
And chase and pit its wits
Against Wesleyans and Congregationalists.

On the chest to avoid litigation,
There was a big white pocket, delicately sewn.
'That', she said, 'is for your handkerchief,
And ever-present comb.
When an opposition forward
Receives a slippery through ball,
Don't play him on, wave handkerchiefs in unison.'
My mother had improved the offside trap;
Even the mighty Arsenal didn't think of that.

Our team are on their knees.
White shirts, as far as the referee can see,
Are wiping tears, with Gascoigne-like ease.
Tomorrow they will play again, on washing lines,
Where the hedgerows used to be.

Stapleford Methodists c.1957/8 Ken's brother, Dennis, front row, second from right, with the ball – and the white-pocketed shirt

At Atcham, by Hotel and Church

If love was ever engineered,
Not just thrilling circumstance,
Then there's a blueprint here,
At Atcham, by hotel and church.
In this benevolent meeting place,
Two bridges ford the snaking river.
Singular, independent, elegant,
In harmony, magnificent.
When their paths cross,
The arches march in measured step,
Take on the road together.
There is just something
Between these two,
When face to face.
Not distance, but room for light,
A necessary breathing space
These lovers grant each other.
Intent, serious, yet,
As lively as the movement of the fishes,
Bright as the kingfisher's flight.
Gracefully they converge,
Ordered, enduring, granite strong,
Crafted and constructed.
James and Hana,
This parallel wonder we celebrate,
Was designed and planned
And engineered by love,
For every stage and span of life.

For James and Hana Beevers   12 November 2016

Owd Chummy

Every Monday morning, at every library, there used to be a tradition known as *The Completion of the Sunday Newspaper Crosswords*. Mr. Spelham was always the first through the doors, *Sunday Express* in hand, entering the sanctuary of the library gratefully, the unfinished clues giving him no rest. The ritual gave him a sense of purpose to start the week. He referred to everyone as 'Chummy', even Shakespeare.

'Have you got Owd Chummy's *Othello*', he said to me one day. 'I need the name of the main protagonist, four letters.' He would have given anything to have his own set of encyclopedias. 'It would be like having me own wheels, Ken.'

He went to the Veterans Club at lunchtime for a drink which, if things were proving difficult, always got him back on the right lines.

Several others usually joined him in the library and they conferred in the reference room. This was their playing field. Dark and oak-panelled, like a Victorian mill manager's office, the solid wooden tables bisecting the room resembled the gridlines of a crossword puzzle itself.

One Monday, a few summers ago, there were half a dozen in, four across the middle by the dictionaries and two down by the atlases. In addition, in the corner by the encyclopedias was a young man, dressed enigmatically in black, looking just like a shaded square, searching for answers of a different kind. The silent concentration was only punctuated by the pleasant rhythmic thud of reference books being set down on oak. Suddenly, there was a loud crash and the clatter of a chair falling over on the wooden floor. Mr. Spelham came rushing out to get me.

Clearly agitated, he exclaimed, 'There's a body in the library! Young Chummy's on the floor, stretched out unconscious', adding cryptically, 'and we can't get to the encyclopedias.' When I got to him, he was just coming round and trying to talk, but at first what he was saying didn't make any sense. 'He's talking in anagrams,' Mr. Spelham said, with some admiration. The general opinion was that he was staring at the ceiling just before he keeled over and the only clue seemed to be the title of the book which had been open in front of him: *Thyroid Disease: The Facts*. We helped him to his seat, as he slowly recovered. Being naturally curious, the puzzlers all waited for the riddle to be explained. With the mahogany shelves and leather tomes in the background, and us all gathered round like interested parties in a solicitor's office, he began to set out the facts.

He had, he said, entered the library feeling perfectly well and quite by chance picked up a book on thyroid disease. After reading for a while, he became convinced he too had the symptoms and began to feel sluggish and exhausted. His heart was racing, his skin seemed dry and itchy, and, despite the summer sun, he started to shiver. What's more, uniquely, he seemed to have the symptoms for both an under- and over-active thyroid. Increasingly worried, he followed the instructions on how to carry out a self-diagnosis, which involved tipping his head back and feeling for bulges just below his Adam's apple. This should have been done using a mirror while drinking a glass of water, but, of course, he had neither of these to hand. Blundering amateurishly on, he must have accidentally squeezed some vital pressure point, causing him to pass out instantaneously. He then fell off his chair and banged his head on a radiator, knocking himself momentarily unconscious. As he finished the story, he smiled weakly.

He could laugh at himself but he still looked pale, worried, tired and unkempt. Despite the comic circumstances, the overall effect was depressing and everyone just sadly sidled away, apart from Mr. Spelham, who took me to one side.

'Young Chummy', he confided, 'drinks in the Veterans Club and is always a bit over-anxious.'

The casualty refused offers of medical assistance but did agree to me giving him a lift home, the only help he'd accept. He thanked me, jumped out of the car and skipped down the path like the man they could not hang, glad to be alive.

Then Mr. Spelham went missing, and for a few weeks was only seen at Asda. I wondered if the incident at the library and the sudden interruption of his familiar routine had made him think. He always said that his pursuit of the prize crossword was an addiction; maybe it didn't seem as important now. But one Monday morning, he resurfaced, striding purposefully in to report back and explain his absence. He'd bought some encyclopedias from Young Chummy, who had become afraid of the power of the printed word. For a while it had been enjoyable, just looking things up at home.

'It's been a real change, a break from routine, a kind of holiday, but I've missed the library. *Britannica*'s just for bedtime reading from now on.'

'Magnus,' I said, for I was allowed to call him by his nickname, 'you really are a bit of a conundrum.' He smiled as if I had paid him a huge compliment. I don't think he could have been happier if he had won the prize crossword itself.

Stanley Has an Off Day

Stanley the Shore Crab lived in Brixham harbour. He had one stalky eye like a periscope and his shell was scarred from wrestling. He loved the crabbing season when the children gathered on the harbour wall and tried to catch him with fishing lines loaded with food. He didn't mind how many times he was caught and liked to be tempted by pieces of squid before making the thrilling ride to the top. It was exciting when it was windy and sometimes he played the fool and fell off on purpose. To make children laugh, the crabs attempted world records and once eighteen of them got on one line. Children loved to catch Stanley because he was old and famous. Before being put gently back in the sea, he always enjoyed a rest in a bucket and maybe a wrestle with Geronimo or Carapace Kate, although usually they just chatted by drumming their pincers.

Tap, tap. 'Nice day for crabbing, Stanley.'

This year the winter was cold, the sea didn't warm up and the crabs slept right through the Easter holidays. The children peered over the wall and shouted for Stanley. From underwater their eyes looked like giant marbles and their faces wobbled like jelly on the moving surface of the sea but Stanley and the other crabs didn't notice. The children went home fed up and some of the grown-ups said they would go to a place called Cromer next year, because it was better for crabs.

The Mayor was very worried but he had an idea. Just after the crabs had been seen moving about, he stood on the harbour wall at the crabbing spot, his big golden chain reflecting in the water, and welcomed them back, explaining it wasn't their fault they had overslept. 'You are very important and Brixham needs you', he said. 'We are going to give the children the best bait – smelly old bacon and frozen squid – free every day all summer. No more Jaffa Cakes and bits of worm for you. Enjoy yourselves.'

Tap, tap. 'Yummy, yummy.'

The news spread. The next day, crabs were queuing up as lines loaded with streaky, lean, smoked, unsmoked and best back bacon, all of it extremely pongy, descended into the sea.

Stanley was embarrassed when he heard he had overslept and missed the school holidays. The cold sea was also making him feel unwell, and all he could do was watch.

'What's up, Stanley?' said Oliver the Octopus.

'I can't walk sideways in a straight line. I'm feeling a bit leggy.'

'You should try being me. I can't keep my legs under control. They've got a mind of their own these tentacles.'

'You don't look well, Stanley' said Horace the Hermit Crab.

'I didn't feel like coming out of my hiding hole today.'

'You should try being me', said Horace.

'Before you ask,' Stanley said to the Mussel Brothers, 'I'm not feeling strong today.'

'You're feeling a bit flat, Stanley? You should try being me', said Freddie the Flounder.

After a while though, Stanley took a fancy to a bit of squid, and he thought he heard his name being called. When he got to the top, he found that a hungry-looking man had caught him. 'Hello, Stanley,' he said, 'or should I say Hello, Sandwich.' Terry the Sandwich Tern just happened to be flying over, saw what was happening and dive-bombed, causing the man to drop the bucket and let Stanley escape.

'You saved my life. He called me a sandwich', said Stanley.

'You should try being me', said Terry.

A Secret Love

At the foot of Helsby Hill,
All Cheshire lies,
Smooth, infinite, tranquil,
Like a perfect love.

On this sandstone outcrop,
Another kind hides,
Awkward, crumbling, dark and numbing,
Forever on the rocks.

At the top, where it's steep and lumpy,
In a maelstrom of longing,
Someone has carved,
'I LOVE MRS CRUMPLEY'.
A formal declaration of infatuation,
A statement scraped on an escarpment
In desperation by an unknown mason,
A life upended, a love suspended,
Unrequited and crushed.

Where are you now, Mrs. Crumpley?
If Paul Simon had sauntered up
This sandy ground,
Seeking relaxation,
After composing *Homeward Bound*
Sat at nearby Widnes Station,
There'd be a song for you,
Imagining your comeliness,
Your vulnerable, endearing crumpliness.

Once, it was a secret love.
Now, it can be seen from Wales,
The Cheshire plain,
From planes above
And, something unforeseen,
All round the world
On a computer screen.

There's a photograph
On the internet
That's been copyrighted.
But you can't copyright love,
Even one wedded in bedrock,
And embedded in wedlock.
I love you too,
Mrs. Crumpley.

© Steve Deer Fine Art Photography

The World's Best Haiku

The world's best haiku
Is not by Matsuo Bashō,
The haiku laureate, who wrote
The most famous poem in Japan:
About pond, frog
And the sound of water.

Nor is it by any of his compatriots:
It isn't even Japanese,
This miniature masterpiece,
Though it's intricately layered
Like delicate netsuke.

It's not written by Confucius,
The greatest slogan writer,
And it's not by Alfred Wainwright,
The famous Lakeland walker,
Who illuminated nature
In loving letters to the fells,
As exquisite as the *Book of Kells*.

You won't find it in *The Rattle Bag*
Or *The Nation's Favourite* anthologies,
It's not in *Poems on the Underground*,
Because it's not considered poetry,
Despite its perfect symmetry
And seventeen-strong syllables,
Which put our shared experience
In context so dramatically.

It wasn't written down.
It was uttered *in situ*,
Spontaneous and improvised,
An off the cuff haiku
Delivered in a silver tongue,
Completely out of the blue,
In a perfect state of Zen,
By the poet Kenneth Wolstenholme,
Informally known as 'Ken'.

Born Worsley 1920, died Torquay 2002.
Accidental author of the world's best haiku:

*Some people are on
the pitch, they think it is all
over. It is now.*

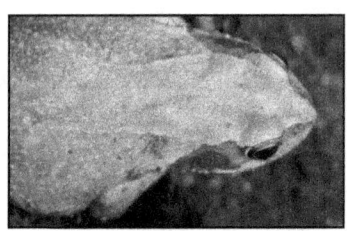

Notes

Page 11   An earlier version of *AQUAMARINE* appeared in *The Broadsheet Issue 4 Autumn 2016* edited by Simon Williams and Susan Taylor.

Page 14   An earlier version of *Slinkers Lane* appeared in *The Manaton Messenger Issue 55 October 2017*. Map Reference SX 755815 Manaton, Devon.

Page 15   Onion Johnnies were Breton farm men and women who travelled to Wales, England and Scotland to sell onions, from 1828 to the late twentieth century. They sailed over in July, returning to Brittany at the end of the year. On 18 November 1905 the SS Hilda sank in bad weather conditions outside Saint-Malo harbour. One hundred and twenty-five people died, including seventy-four Onion Johnnies.

Page 16   The *Cordyline australis*, when established, is quite a tough plant and can stand up to the rigours of the North West weather. The *Torbay Dazzler* has variegated leaves, with creamy white stripes. Walter Greenwood's *Love on the Dole* (1933) is set in Salford.

Page 19   In 1969 my mother worked at Baxter, Woodhouse and Taylor in Poynton, Cheshire. Products, including windcheaters, electric blankets and diving and high altitude flying suits, were sold under the Windak trademark … and space suits, but that was top secret.

Page 21   The aviator is my father-in-law, Roy de Courcy, a World War II pilot, a great man, who is much missed.

Page 22   In Hull and Lincolnshire, tenfoots are alleyways behind the houses, so called because of their approximate width. Philip Larkin described Hull as 'very nice and flat for cycling'. In the 1950s 100,000 people, one third of the population, still rode bicycles regularly.

Page 24   Eager Beaver. An eagre is also a dialect word for the Severn Bore. Ken Dodd was famous for the duration of his shows. 'A watch is no good for you in this show, you need a calendar. We might be finished by Tuesday.' Sir Kenneth Arthur Dodd OBE, 1927-2018, Liverpool gentleman. Thanks for the laughs.

Page 25 Thanks to Simon Pitt, Birmingham Poet Laureate 1999/2000, for the disappearing name and the inspiring workshop with children at Breightmet Library, Bolton, 1989.

Page 28 Bertie Lewis was born in Chicago. Following the outbreak of World War II, he went to England and joined the RAF, serving in 102 Squadron of Bomber Command. He settled in Bolton in 1961. He was a peace campaigner who attended many protests. For many years he held a weekly vigil in Bolton's Victoria Square. A flagstone inlaid with a white poppy was unveiled there on 1 August 2015. At the ceremony he was described as 'a true internationalist who made his home in our town'.

Page 34 Or is it just des(s)erts? One of the named apples is a cooking variety. There are no prizes for identifying the odd one out. We were walking through Crockenwell in Devon.

Page 36 1976 was one of the driest, hottest and sunniest summers of the twentieth century. On the morning of Sunday 9 May, we went to Chudleigh Knighton Heath to hear the nightingale. At that time it was one of only two places in Devon where nightingales bred. Nightingales don't only sing at night. They sing readily by day and are at their loudest in the morning, but after sunset their song is clarified by the reduction in visual and aural distractions. This is why they are associated with love, and 'frolicking', as in the traditional folk song, *One Morning in May*. The last recorded breeding in Devon was in Exeter in 2001 and nightingales are now rare passage migrants.

Page 38 John Charles, 1931-2004, is rated as the greatest all round footballer ever to come from Britain. The Hungarian triangle refers to Ferenc Puskas, Nandor Hidegkuti, and Sandor Kocsis, the stars of the Hungary team who on 25 November 1953 beat England 6-3 at Wembley with a devastating new style of football. Hungary also produced triangular stamps, as catalogued by world famous philatelic specialists Stanley Gibbons.
Written long before January 2019, the Cardiff City goalscoring, flying Bluebird imagery pre-dates the tragic deaths of Emiliano Sala and his pilot, David Ibbotson.

Page 39 Recently, I discovered a fascinating blog, written in February 2017 by renowned poet Martyn Crucefix, entitled *14 Ways to Write an Ekphrastic Poem* (a poem inspired by visual art). There are two extraordinary coincidences in the blog. Four of the techniques are listed under the sub-heading *Through Ventriloquism* and Crucefix cites Michael Longley's poem *Man Lying on a Wall*, inspired by Lowry's painting. Having been previously unaware of Longley's poem and his celebrated book of the same title, I am pleased to have unwittingly followed in his distinguished footsteps, in subject matter at least.

Page 41   The girl who loved the moon's favourite song is *The Girl Who Fell in Love with the Moon* by Boo Hewerdine.

Page 43   *The Battle of Spittle Street* was inspired by a visit to the Devon village of Trusham. On a wall in the centre, there is a plaque with a poem about the village by Charles Causley, the Cornish poet. This was the ancestral home of the Causley family. The village pub, the Cridford Inn, is probably the oldest in Devon and possibly one of the oldest in England.

Page 51   Dag Hammarskjöld served as the second Secretary General of the United Nations from 1953 to his death in a plane crash in September 1961. He was en route to cease-fire negotiations during the Congo Crisis. His book of diary reflections and poetry, *Markings*, was published after his death.
Duncan Edwards was one of the Busby Babes. He died from his injuries two weeks after the Munich air disaster. Hours before his death, the March 1958 issue of *Charles Buchan's Football Monthly* was published with a photograph of a smiling Edwards on the cover. He was much more than a tin god in football boots. There are blue plaques in Dudley and Stretford.

Page 53   At last count, there are fourteen English Heritage plaques in Liverpool and many more provided by Liverpool City Council and the Wavertree Society. The goal net idea occurred to John Brodie while watching a match at Everton in 1889 when a dispute erupted over whether or not the ball had passed through the goalposts. Various clubs claim first use of the goal net but Simon Marland, in his book *Bolton Wanderers FC 1877-2002*, says that goal nets were used for the first time, initially in one half of a friendly game between Nottingham Forest and Bolton Wanderers, in January 1891, and that's good enough for me.

Page 58   The race was the City of Hull Police Sports Marathon, 7 June 1913.

John Noyland, my Grandad, was eighth out of fourteen finishers, completing the twenty mile course in a time of two hours, twenty-four minutes and five seconds. And then the war came.

Page 62   *The Light of the World* is an allegorical painting by the English Pre-Raphaelite artist William Holman Hunt, 1827-1910.

Page 69   A little Byronic poetic licence here, as Marriott Edgar's monologue, immortalised by Stanley Holloway, was originally entitled *The Lion and Albert*.

Page 70   The match was the 1995 Football League Cup Final (Coca-Cola Cup) between Liverpool and Bolton Wanderers. Liverpool won 2 - 1. My brother played for the Stapleford Methodists, in the home-made shirt with the pocket.

Page 79   An earlier version of *The World's Best Haiku* was published in *The Broadsheet Issue 3 Autumn 2015* edited by Simon Williams and Susan Taylor.
Here's another one:
The old stadium.
The ball flies into the net.
The sound of cheering.

Illustrations and Credits

Beevers Family Photos
Front Cover Ken's Mum, Ivy Beevers (second row, left); Front Cover Ken's Dad, Arthur Beevers (second row, right); Front Cover Jacqui Beevers (circle); Pages 19 & 20 Ken's Mum, Ivy Beevers; Page 21 Jacqui's Dad, Roy de Courcy; Page 71 Stapleford Methodists c.1957/8.

Brian Mills Designs www.bmillsdesigns.co.uk
Front Cover Kindly designed by Brian Mills Designs. Brian also created or sourced the elements within the cover design not otherwise attributed in these credits.

Campaign For Nuclear Disarmament
Page 28 Quite deliberately never copyrighted, the famous symbol is kindly made freely available to all by CND.

Hull City Council
Front Cover The famous Three Coronets of Hull, found everywhere around the city, reproduced by courtesy of Hull City Council.

Ian Beech
Front Cover Moon; Front Cover Pilgrim Shell; Back Cover Ken Beevers; Page 40 Ken Beevers Lying on a Wall, 2018; Page 48 Mouse and Candle; Page 54 Goal Net; Page 57 Edith's Diary; Page 59 Ken's Grandfather's Rose Bowl; Page 80 Frog, Crediton, Devon.
(All images © Ian Beech).

Ken Beevers
Front Cover Wintergreen Ointment Tin; Page 14 Parliament Street, Exeter; Page 18 Ken & Jacqui's Sons Gavin (left) and James; Page 29 The Bertie Lewis Flagstone, Victoria Square, Bolton; Page 54 Goalposts on a Wall, Bolton; Page 60 Cecil Road Milk Bottle, Paignton; Page 76 Brixham.
(All images © Ken Beevers).

Liverpool City Council
Front Cover Image of John Brodie from the May 1906 edition of *The Guild Gazette* (Magazine of the Liverpool Municipal Officers' Guild) kindly supplied courtesy of Liverpool Record Office, Liverpool Libraries (top row, right).

Royal Mail Group Limited
Back Cover John Charles stamp reproduced by kind permission of Royal Mail Group Limited. Stamp design © Royal Mail Group Limited.

Soccer Attic Ltd
Front Cover Copyright picture of Duncan Edwards reproduced by courtesy of Soccer Attic Ltd. (top row, left).

Steve Deer Fine Art Photography
Page 78 I LOVE MRS CRUMPLEY This monochrome version of Steve Deer's copyright image reproduced by kind permission of Steve Deer Fine Art Photography.

Many thanks to all of the above for their contributions, helping bring this book to publication.

Every effort has been made to locate owners of any copyright material used in this book. The author apologises for any omissions. Those brought to the author's attention will be incorporated in future editions.

About the Author

Ken Beevers was born in Hull, in the final fading hour of the last kick of November, after his mother had eaten fish and chips. It was a Saturday, so at least there was some jollity in the air.

He is a former librarian, who lived in Torquay in the 1970s, working for Torbay Library Service and then Devon Libraries. He moved to Paignton in 2011, after working for Bolton Library and Museum Services, and living in Bolton, the friendliest of northern towns, for thirty-three years. He was a regular Father Christmas, a reluctant Eric the Owl, and once was Postman Pat for a whole week. He also worked in the Local History Centre, sharing the top job in poetry – responsibility for the care of Walt Whitman's stuffed canary, the subject of Whitman's poem, *My Canary Bird*, and one of Bolton Library and Museum Services' most prized possessions. There is no greater calling.

He developed a love for Bolton and its history, wrote two books, and gave talks, especially promoting the life and work of Bolton's most famous author, Bill Naughton, whose archive the library service acquired in 2000. Ken worked on local history and Heritage Lottery projects, and was Secretary of a local history society for thirty years. He also taught local history classes for the Workers' Educational Association. Together with his love of football and walking, all this may seem irrelevant as far as poetry is concerned, but the influences are there. He claims his favourite poet is Welsh football legend, John Toshack (*Gosh it's Tosh*, 1976) but he may wish to reconsider that …

Retiring to Torbay, the Devon effect encouraged him to do something creative, so he enrolled on a writing course at Paignton Library run by South Devon College Adult and Community Learning Service, and taught by Sam Watson. He was encouraged by third place in the College poetry competition, and the constructive feedback. After regular visits to the Blue Walnut Cafe, Torquay, for the monthly poetry nights at Poetry Island, he did a course in performance poetry there, run by Chris Brooks in June 2014. Eventually he performed on its gentle shores, encouraged by the then host Robert Garnham, and later by Ian Beech, the host from 2014 to 2017. He has also performed at other Devon venues. He is a regular at Stanza Extravaganza at the Artizan Gallery, and at Big Poetry at the Blue Walnut, the successor to Poetry Island.

Poems by Ken have featured in *The Broadsheet*, an annual anthology of South West poets, edited by Susan Taylor and Simon Williams. Except for one story, everything in this book was written in Devon, prompted by homework, or for performance at Poetry Island.

Ken Beevers has a unique voice. Gentle and masculine, witty and poignant, romantic and down-to-earth, he has a keenly observant eye for quirky details, a touching honesty in his personal recollections, and warm empathy for the human condition.

A story-telling poet, Ken loves the richness of words, yet he mostly uses everyday language, threaded on rhythm and rhyme, to draw us into his deceptively simple, multi-layered poems. There is always humour, quite often there is a delicately-sketched sadness, especially in his sideways glance at family memories that ache and entertain in equal measure.

And there is love. Romantic love, expressed with sensitive sensuality, and family love, love of history, of the countryside and of Northern towns, of football, books and music, of underdogs and misfits. Like his tramp with a trolley on the Manchester Road, Ken himself is always *'Recycling gold'*.

AQUAMARINE will take you from the sea to the moon and back, via Hull and the *Liverpool Echo*. Let Ken show you *'what a bit of Larkin leads to'* and follow him down *Slinkers Lane*, *'Which twists and turns and twists again'* – it's a journey full of surprises, and richly rewarding.

Elaine Jarvest Miller

There is a gentleness in Beevers' work that sits you down by the fire and draws you into his experience of a world now largely lost. But don't get too comfortable for he will catch you with a turn that stops you in your tracks or trips you up with unexpected humour. He also has an innate ability to weave lyricism throughout his work that makes the poems flow effortlessly. This is a collection that will continually delight, no matter how many times it is read.

Paul Mortimer

Ken Beevers dances with language and takes the listener to places we recognise yet see afresh. His mix of autobiography and humour is a constant delight. An earnest, softly-spoken, calm-mannered giant of the West Country poetry scene.

Robert Garnham

Ken Beevers' *AQUAMARINE* is tender, insightful and funny. His love of language and reading is tracked throughout the book, opening with the title poem and its enjoyment of words. Poignantly too, the poem *I Was Reading* shows his journey of discovery through literature.

In *The Secret Seamstress* we meet his mother, who sewed many things, including, (secretly), spacesuits for NASA. This is a wonderful poem, unexpected, well-crafted, with the language carefully echoing a seamstress' skill. We learn that she added to Neil Armstrong's suit '... *a secret stitch/The quality checker never found,/A lucky thread to keep him safe,* ...'. A very special seamstress, a lovely poem.

In *Illumination*, Ken reveals how he began to write poetry, as well as his quiet, Yorkshire humour. Perhaps his self-deprecating, yet insightful style is best shown in the poem *Man Lying on a Wall, 1957, By L. S. Lowry*, another fascinating, well-made poem.

I am so pleased that with *AQUAMARINE*, Ken Beevers can share his poems and stories with their particular humour and gentle observations.

Rose Cook

Ken Beevers captivates audiences with his charming, poignant poetry, often vividly evoking bygone days. He's a master storyteller. You'll hang on his every word.

Ian Beech

Also available from Poetry Island Press

Ian Beech *On the Road to Ollantaytambo*   978-0-9933961-0-6

www.ingramcontent.com/pod-product-compliance
Lightning Source LLC
Chambersburg PA
CBHW071732040426
42446CB00011B/2326